MARY
Queen *of* Scots

The Infant Queen

MARY'S LIFE started in tragedy: as she was born in the Palace of Linlithgow, her father, James V, lay dying in Falkland Palace. He had collapsed, broken-hearted after the defeat of his army by the English at Solway Moss. Nor was he cheered by the news of Mary's birth: 'Adieu, farewell, it came with a lass, it will pass with a lass.'

He was referring to the fact that his family, the Stewarts, had come to the throne in Scotland through the marriage of Marjorie Bruce, daughter of King Robert the Bruce, to Walter Stewart. James had good reason to worry about his throne passing not just to a woman, but to 'a very weak child, and not likely to live as it is thought': many Scottish lords had royal links and were ready to claim the throne. Six days after Mary's birth, James died. Contrary to expectation, however, Mary became strong and healthy and was crowned queen when she was less than a year old.

Almost at once the question arose: to whom should the infant Mary be betrothed? Her future husband would eventually take power in Scotland and Henry VIII of England, eager to unite the two countries, pressed for a union with his five-year-old son, Edward. Some Scottish lords supported his cause, but most favoured a marriage within the 'auld alliance' to the newborn French prince. (For 200 years Scotland and France had joined forces to help each other against England's expansionist ambitions.) Henry was furious. He invaded Scotland to enforce his will in what was called the 'Rough Wooing'. Mary, now five years old, was sent to France for safety and the French king Henry II despatched soldiers to Scotland to protect the country.

MARY OF GUISE

Mary's mother was born and brought up in France. Her brothers, Francis, Duke of Guise, and Charles, Cardinal of Lorraine, eager to advance their own fortunes, sought a marriage alliance between the infant Mary Queen of Scots and the French dauphin.

PALACE OF LINLITHGOW
*Mary was born in the palace of Linlithgow on
8 December 1542, probably in the upper room, the
queen's bed-chamber, in the north-west tower.
The once splendid palace is now in ruins.*

MARY STUART'S FAMILY TREE
*The Scottish and English royal houses were linked by the
marriage of Margaret Tudor to James IV. This link later
formed the basis of Mary's claim to the English throne.*

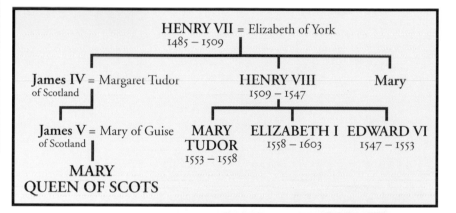

HENRY VII = Elizabeth of York
1485 – 1509

James IV = Margaret Tudor
of Scotland

HENRY VIII
1509 – 1547

Mary

James V = Mary of Guise
of Scotland

**MARY
TUDOR**
1553 – 1558

ELIZABETH I
1558 – 1603

EDWARD VI
1547 – 1553

**MARY
QUEEN OF SCOTS**

INCHMAHOME PRIORY
*When English troops
invaded Scotland in
1544 and burned
Holyroodhouse Palace in
Edinburgh, Mary took
refuge in Inchmahome
Priory. Built on an island
in the middle of the Lake
of Menteith, it was easier
to defend than many
other castles.*

JAMES V
*Mary's father, James V,
was the son of James IV
and Margaret Tudor,
sister of Henry VIII of
England. Henry wanted
to strengthen the links
between the Scottish and
English thrones by marry-
ing his son Edward to
the infant Mary.*

French Childhood

MARY'S CHILDHOOD in France was happy and luxurious. She joined the royal nursery and was treated as befitted the future queen of France and Scotland. Mary was a captivating child – pretty, intelligent and vivacious. The French already regarded her as a brave and romantic heroine, who had fled from the bleakness of Scotland for protection against the English. She soon learned to speak French, and it became her first language.

Mary was loved and pampered. Henry II, the French king, said of her, 'The little Queen of Scots is the most perfect child that I have ever seen.' She enjoyed the splendour of the French royal palaces and learned to speak Italian, Spanish and Latin, to sew tapestries, write poetry and play musical instruments. For the rest of her life she would love riding and hunting, skills she learned in the countryside around Fontainebleau and the many other palaces that the royal nursery frequented. But, as the intended wife of the future king, she learned nothing of politics or government.

Mary of Guise, who remained in Scotland as one of its regents, was deeply upset to be separated from her daughter and the high point of Mary's childhood was a visit from her in 1550. The seven-year-old Mary wrote to her grandmother that the visit was 'the greatest happiness which I could wish for in this world.' Mary of Guise stayed in France for a year and her daughter's affection remained so strong that, when her mother died ten years later, Mary collapsed with grief.

After the French royal children joined the court in 1553, Mary spent more time with her Guise relations. Her education was supervised by the cardinal of Guise who, unusually at that time, encouraged tolerance between Roman Catholics and Protestants. The Cardinal's teachings influenced Mary, a strict Roman Catholic, when she later returned to Protestant Scotland.

MARY, AGED NINE
This crayon drawing was commissioned by Catherine de Medici, queen of France, in addition to drawings of her own children and shows Mary with child-like features but royal bearing. Mary was treated with the same respect, care and lavishness as the French royal children.

PALACE OF FONTAINEBLEAU

The chateaux and palaces in which Mary lived were magnificent examples of Renaissance splendour. They included galleries of paintings and exquisite furnishings. Italian and French architects and designers contributed to the building of the Palace of Fontainebleau.

DELICATE NEEDLEWORK

This tapestry, worked by Mary, is a monogram of the letters of her name, Maria S. Although most of the existing tapestries worked by her were completed when she was a prisoner in England, they show the exquisite stitching she learned as a child in France.

LETTER TO HER MOTHER

Mary wrote to her mother throughout her childhood. Although she never forgot the language of Scotland, she always wrote in French and signed herself 'MARIE'. She also changed the spelling of her name to the French Stuart.

PRINCE FRANCIS

The dauphin was one year younger than Mary and the two grew up together as brother and sister. Francis was a pale, frail child who looked younger than he was and often suffered from ill health.

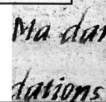

Queen Consort of France

WHEN MARY was 15 and Francis just over 14, they were married with great splendour and ceremony in the Cathedral of Notre Dame in Paris in April 1558. Francis was small for his age, shy and sullen. Mary was beautiful and elegant and Francis adored her – she was a childhood friend and one of the few people he felt at ease with. Mary was very fond of him too, but it probably never occurred to her to question the marriage – it had been destined for her for as long as she could remember.

Seven months after the wedding in Notre Dame, the English queen Mary Tudor died, prompting Henry II of France and some English Catholics to claim that Mary Queen of Scots was the rightful successor to the English throne. Elizabeth, the Protestant daughter of Anne Boleyn, was illegitimate, they said, and could not inherit the throne and, thereafter, Mary and Francis carried the royal arms of England, as well as those of France and Scotland.

The following year Henry II himself died in a jousting accident and Mary became Queen of France. Her reign in France was short however: Francis was not strong and in December 1560 he developed an ear infection and died. Mary was grief-stricken, but, for the first time, she was in a position to decide her own future. She first considered a political marriage to Don Carlos, the heir to the Spanish throne, but, after negotiations with the government of Scotland, she decided to return to the land of her birth. She sadly said goodbye to France and set sail for Scotland. In so doing she exchanged her familiar and civilised life for the rough and ready, and sometimes violent, world of Scotland's nobles.

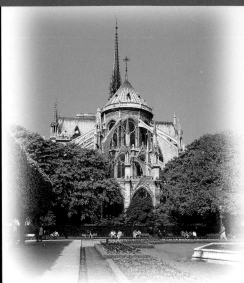

NOTRE DAME CATHEDRAL
Mary Queen of Scots and the dauphin
Francis were married in Notre Dame
Cathedral. Henry II and Catherine de
Medici spared no expense and it was
attended by the French cardinals and
nobility. Afterwards there was a royal
ball followed by 'a supper of such
magnificence that none of the servants
there had ever seen the like.'

HUSBAND AND WIFE
Mary with her husband, Francis, dauphin of France.
This painting from a miniature in Catherine de
Medici's prayer book probably flatters Francis,
since Mary was almost certainly taller than him.
Mary's beauty was legendary: 'the eyes of this
Queen suffice to light up the whole sea with their
lovely fire', wrote the poet Châtelard.

DEATH OF HENRY II

This deathbed scene is a detail from a woodcut by Tortorel and Perrissin. With Henry's death, Mary Queen of Scots, who is shown just to the left of the right-hand bedpost, became queen of France.

CORONATION OF ELIZABETH I

Elizabeth was crowned queen of England in 1558. She later became one of England's greatest monarchs, but at first she was considered stubborn and frivolous. In contrast, when the English ambassador Sir Nicholas Throckmorton had an interview with Mary in France in 1560, he was impressed by her wisdom and modesty.

QUEEN CLAIMANT OF ENGLAND

Mary's claim to the English throne was based on the fact that her grandmother, Margaret Tudor, was the sister of Henry VIII, while those who did not recognise Henry VIII's divorce from Catherine of Aragon declared that Elizabeth, the daughter of his second marriage, was illegitimate. In July 1560, Mary acknowledged that Elizabeth was the rightful ruler of England, but the childless Elizabeth would never forget that Mary was her legitimate heir and had once claimed her throne.

WIDOW IN MOURNING

In France, white was the colour of mourning. In the space of two years, Mary lost her father-in-law, husband and mother, and when she sailed to Scotland she left behind the country she knew best. During the voyage to Scotland, Mary wrote a poem which began 'Farewell my beautiful France, my dearest homeland'.

Mary Returns to Scotland

THE SCOTLAND Mary returned to was very different from the country she had left 13 years earlier. While Mary, a staunch Roman Catholic, was growing up in Catholic France, Scotland had become Protestant. In the 1540s George Wishart and others spread the ideas and beliefs of the Protestant movement and, in 1559, John Knox returned to Scotland from Switzerland to preach ever more vehemently. With his fierce encouragement, a group of Scottish Protestant nobles, known as the Lords of the Congregation, overthrew Mary of Guise's government and set up a Protestant parliament.

Before Mary returned to Scotland her illegitimate half-brother, the Earl of Moray, came to France to pave the way for her return and to negotiate the terms: if Mary agreed to accept the changes made by the Protestants to Parliament and the Scottish church, she would be allowed to follow her own religion in private.

The Earl of Moray continued to advise Mary during the early years of her reign in Scotland. She soon captured the hearts of the Scottish people who warmed to her beauty and sympathised with her plight as a widow. As time went on, they were relieved and reassured by her attitude of tolerance towards the new Protestant Church.

One person who was not prepared to accept Mary or her faith, however, was John Knox and he did not mince his words. 'One mass is more fearful than 10,000 armed enemies being landed in any part of the realm,' he thundered. He tried in vain to convert Mary to Protestantism and often spoke out against her 'evil ways'. But, rail as he might, it was not John Knox that brought about Mary's downfall in 1567.

MARY ARRIVES AT LEITH
When Mary's ship docked at Leith, she was welcomed by a sympathetic but cautious crowd of people. How would a Roman Catholic queen, they wondered, react to the Protestantism which had swept Scotland?

MARTYRDOM OF GEORGE WISHART
In 1546 George Wishart was tried by Cardinal Beaton and condemned to burn at the stake for preaching the Protestant beliefs. Wishart's death, however, rallied more people to the Protestant cause, including his friend John Knox.

JOHN KNOX (1513–72)

In the 1540s, John Knox, a Roman Catholic priest, became involved in the Protestant movement. After the murder of Cardinal Beaton, Knox joined the assassins in St Andrew's Castle. The castle was captured by French soldiers in 1547, and Knox served 19 months as a galley slave, and then the next 10 years in exile in England and in Switzerland, where he was much influenced by John Calvin, the Protestant leader. He returned to Scotland in 1559.

JAMES STEWART, EARL OF MORAY

The Earl of Moray was Mary's elder half-brother. He paved the way for her return to Scotland and advised her in the early years of her rule. His sound advice ensured a peaceful transition of power and Mary's acceptance by the Scottish people.

JOHN KNOX'S 'FIRST BLAST'

A contemporary woodcut shows John Knox blowing a trumpet against 'the Monstrous Regiment of Women'. It is based on a piece of invective Knox wrote against the right of women to rule, entitled 'First Blast'. Although Mary Queen of Scots is shown in the woodcut, the First Blast was published in 1558 and directed at the Catholic rulers, Mary of Guise in Scotland and Mary Tudor of England.

JOHN KNOX'S MEETING WITH MARY

In September 1561 John Knox met Mary for the first time and tried to persuade her to give up Roman Catholicism and convert to the Scottish Protestant church. Mary refused and had many heated arguments with him.

Mary's Scotland

MARY LEFT the sophisticated and luxurious palaces and chateaux of France to return to the cold, bleak country of Scotland. Instead of elegant, spacious rooms she came to turreted stone castles. Holyroodhouse Palace was the exception. The Palace was architecturally closer to its French counterparts than anywhere else in Scotland, mainly because her father had employed several French masons when he extended the original tower, and her French mother, Mary of Guise, had been living there before her.

Due to the 'auld alliance' there were many trade and cultural links with France. Indeed, most French people regarded Scotland as a rather bleak and unsophisticated province of France. Mary tried to recreate much of her French life in Scotland. She introduced into court life the entertainments and pleasures she had enjoyed in France – music, dancing, banquets, cards, dice and plays. She had a private chapel at Holyroodhouse in which she continued to celebrate Mass. John Knox abominated her way of life as 'offensive in the sight of God'. He even claimed that a famine in 1563 was sent by God as a punishment: 'The riotous festivity and huge banquets in the palace provoked God into this action'.

Mary continued to hunt and hawk, as she had in France. She rode in the magnificent parks around Holyroodhouse and Falkland Palace. She even played golf. She brought French servants with her and an Italian secretary called David Rizzio.

Although Mary spent much of her time at Holyroodhouse, she also travelled around her realm and had castles at Stirling and Linlithgow.

JOHN KNOX HOUSE

John Knox House, where Knox is believed to have lived for a while, is about halfway between Holyroodhouse Palace and Edinburgh Castle so that Mary would have passed it every time she travelled between the two. It is small compared to many Edinburgh houses of the time. Land was so scarce within the city walls that most houses were several storeys high.

EDINBURGH IN 1582

Overlooked by Edinburgh Castle on its volcanic mound, 16th-century Edinburgh was a walled city of no more than 9,000 people. Holyroodhouse Palace lay outside the walls to the east and Edinburgh's main thoroughfare, the High Street, linked the palace to the castle. To the north, where Princes Street Gardens are now situated, was a large natural moat – the Nor Loch.

MARY'S HARP

Mary loved music and played several instruments, including this Highland harp. It is decorated with scrolls and animals.

THE PALACE OF HOLYROODHOUSE

The palace as it was about 100 years after Mary lived there. The building she knew was extended and improved, but Mary's own rooms and bedchamber survive to this day.

QUEEN MARY'S ROOM IN HOLYROODHOUSE

Mary lived in the same rooms as her mother, Mary of Guise, had done before her. This sketch of her room was made in about 1854 and is from Swarbreck's 'Sketches in Scotland'.

Marriage to Darnley

THERE WAS NO DOUBT in anyone's mind that Mary would marry again, if only to provide an heir. Her husband, however, would in effect gain the throne of Scotland and suitors came from all over Europe, from Sweden, Spain and England. Since Mary was the official heir to the English throne, Elizabeth was particularly anxious for her to marry someone who would benefit England. Mary, however, threw political considerations aside when she fell in love with her cousin, Henry Stuart, Lord Darnley.

Few people approved of Mary's choice – not John Knox, for Darnley was Catholic, nor her advisor, Lord James Stewart, the Earl of Moray who rebelled and fled to England. Elizabeth too was furious, since Lord Darnley was also a grandson of Margaret Tudor and so strengthened Mary's claim to the English throne. Mary did not care. She was so in love with Darnley that she did not realise that behind the elegant good-looks lay a vain, selfish, weak man who was interested only in furthering his own position. Marrying Darnley was Mary's great mistake and the beginning of her demise.

The marriage took place at Holyrood on 29 July 1565, but by 1566, when Mary was pregnant with Darnley's child, the love affair was already waning. In addition, Darnley had become bitterly jealous of Mary's secretary, David Rizzio, with whom she often played cards until late at night. In March 1566 Darnley, with a group of conspirators, murdered Rizzio in the Queen's apartments in Holyroodhouse. The murder destroyed any remaining love that Mary had for Darnley, and Mary afterwards believed that Darnley had intended to threaten her own life too. She waited, however, until her child was born in June 1566 before she acted.

HENRY STUART AND MARY QUEEN OF SCOTS
This picture of Mary with her husband Henry Stuart, Lord Darnley, is from a contemporary manuscript, the Seton Armorial. Darnley was vain, charming and ambitious. Mary fell passionately in love with him, but he wanted the trappings of power without the responsibilities.

DAVID RIZZIO
(d. 1566)
Mary employed Rizzio as her secretary in 1564 to deal with her correspondence in French and with the Pope. He was a talented musician who soon became a close and trusted companion to Mary. Their shared love of music led Mary to spend many long evenings with Rizzio, fuelling Darnley's jealousy and provoking distrust and resentment amongst the nobles.

MURDER OF RIZZIO
This 18th-century painting by John Opie shows the murder of Rizzio in the Queen's apartments in Holdyroodhouse Palace. Darnley was present when a group of nobles dragged Rizzio out of the room and stabbed him to death.

MARY WITH HER SON JAMES VI
Mary, already pregnant with Darnley's child when Rizzio was murdered, gave birth to a son, James, in Edinburgh Castle in 1566. This portrait was painted in 1583 by an unknown artist from his imagination: James was taken away from his 'unsuitable' mother when he was 10 months old and Mary never saw her son again.

Darnley's Murder

RIZZIO'S MURDER solved nothing: Mary and Darnley became further estranged and Mary turned for help and support to the Earl of Moray, now returned from England, and the Earl of Bothwell. Late in November 1566, Mary discussed with them the possibility of divorce and dark hints were made of 'other means', but there is no real evidence that Mary was ever involved in Darnley's murder.

Nevertheless around 2 am on 10 February 1567 the house at Kirk o' Field in Edinburgh, where Darnley was recuperating from an illness, was destroyed by gunpowder. The crack of the explosion woke Mary, asleep at Holyroodhouse. Strangely, Darnley was not killed by the blast: something must have disturbed him and he escaped into nearby gardens. There his semi-naked, strangled body was found with that of his servant. Mary's immediate reactions were shock, outrage and alarm. Since she too had been in the house a few hours earlier, she thought the explosion had been aimed at her. It soon became apparent, however, that Bothwell was responsible. He was brought to trial in Edinburgh in April, but he filled the city with 4,000 of his men and was acquitted.

Now sure of his power, Bothwell wooed Mary. She refused him, but, as she returned to Edinburgh after visiting her 10-month-old son in Stirling in April 1567, he intercepted her and tricked her into accompanying him to his castle at Dunbar. There he 'ravished her and laid with her against her will'. How Mary really felt about Bothwell is unclear, but she agreed to marry him in a Protestant wedding service which took place at Holyroodhouse on 15 May, just three months after Darnley's murder. Mary's reputation was now in tatters: her marriage to her husband's murderer scandalised the nation.

*JAMES HEPBURN, EARL OF BOTHWELL
Painted in 1566, this is the only known portrait of the Earl of Bothwell. He was a violent, ambitious nobleman, who, with the help of several other nobles, most likely murdered Darnley in the hope of securing the throne for himself.*

*HERMITAGE CASTLE
Hermitage Castle, 12 miles south of Hawick. While staying in Jedburgh, Mary, accompanied by the Earl of Moray and members of her court, rode to Hermitage Castle to visit Bothwell, who was ill. The visit is sometimes used to imply that Mary was in love with Bothwell, but there is no evidence that the visit was romantic rather than official.*

MARY QUEEN OF SCOT'S HOUSE, JEDBURGH

Mary stayed in this house when she came to Jedburgh in October 1566 to preside over the local justice court. After riding 20 miles over the moors and back to Hermitage Castle, she caught a fever and nearly died here. The French ambassador, however, blamed the illness on 'heartbreak' due to Darnley's misuse of her.

MARY'S POCKET WATCH

During her ride to see Bothwell, Mary lost her watch in a bog now called Queen's Mire. This 16th-century French pocket watch was discovered in the Mire by a shepherd 250 years later.

SKETCH OF DARNLEY'S MURDER

The exact circumstances of Darnley's murder are a mystery. This contemporary sketch shows the house at Kirk o' Field after the explosion with the bodies of Darnley and his servant in a nearby field (top right). In the top left is Darnley's son in his cradle, while (bottom left) Darnley's body is carried away.

CRUDE PROPAGANDA

Many Scottish people thought that Mary was implicated in Darnley's death. This placard, which appeared in Edinburgh soon after the murder, shows Mary as a mermaid (a symbol for prostitution) above a circle of daggers surrounding a hare (Bothwell's family crest).

Mary Abdicates

IT IS DIFFICULT to know what Mary's real feelings for Bothwell were. Had she been forced into marriage with him or had she willingly agreed? She was jealously dominated by him, but she was not prepared to leave him to save her reputation and appease the growing hostility towards ▮▮▮ The matter came to a head on 15 June 1567. An army of opposing nobles confronted Bothwell, Mary and her army at Carberry Hill.

Bothwell retreated and Mary was 'escorted' back to Edinburgh and then imprisoned in Lochleven Castle. Mary's spirit was broken. On 24 July she was forced to abdicate in favour of her infant son, James, and to name as Regent her half-brother, the Earl of Moray. Bothwell fled to Denmark where he was kept in solitary confinement and died, insane, in 1578.

The castle on Lochleven was bleak, isolated and thought to be impregnable. But 10 months after her arrival there, Mary managed to escape. She enlisted the help of Willie Douglas, a young member of the household, and his brother. Between them, they managed ▮▮ get the keys of the castle gate from the governor and smuggled Mary out, dressed as a servant, to a waiting boat.

Mary headed west where most of her supporters were. At Langside near Glasgow, however, her army was intercepted and routed by Moray's forces. Mary fled south to Dumfries to take stock of her position. Why did she then decide to seek help from her cousin Elizabeth in England? Her advisors urged her to hide in Scotland, or, better still, to flee to France. The government of France would have been sure to help a Catholic queen against a Protestant uprising. The Guise family would have supported her and, as Queen Dowager, she had property and wealth there. Yet, without invitation, she chose to throw herself on the mercy of Elizabeth, the Protestant queen whose throne she had once claimed.

BATTLE OF CARBERRY HILL
Carberry Hill was the site of a bloodless confrontation between Mary Queen of Scots and the Earl of Bothwell against the forces of a group of Scottish lords. Bothwell retreated to Dunbar Castle and, as shown in the centre of the picture, Mary was led away on horseback by the Scottish lords.

LOCHLEVEN CASTLE
Two years after spending her honeymoon with Darnley at Lochleven Castle, Mary returned, but this time as a prisoner. She was held here for nearly a year before she managed to escape.

JAMES VI

On 29 July 1567 James, the young son of Mary and Darnley, was crowned king of Scotland at Stirling. The following month, the Earl of Moray was proclaimed Regent, making him the person who, in the end, gained most from the debacle of Mary's unfortunate marriages and their consequences. James never saw his mother after 1567 and was brought up in Stirling Castle in the Protestant religion.

MINIATURE OF MARY QUEEN OF SCOTS

Although Mary was disgraced by her marriage to Bothwell, some people remained loyal to her. Nicholas Hilliard painted this miniature of Mary between 1575 and 1580, probably for the benefit of her supporters while she was in prison.

Imprisonment in England

ALTHOUGH MARY innocently assumed that her cousin, Queen Elizabeth, would help her, Elizabeth did not trust the woman who had once claimed her throne. Indeed Elizabeth felt safer with the infant James on the Scottish throne, but she could not support the overthrow of a rightful queen. It might encourage others to do the same in England! What was Elizabeth to do with her unwanted guest?

By October 1568 Elizabeth had decided to hold Mary in England while English commissioners held an enquiry into Darnley's death. If Mary was found to have been involved in the murder she would be returned to Scotland. During the enquiry, the Scottish lords produced a casket of incriminating letters, which they alleged Mary had written to Bothwell. Although unconvinced by the letters, Elizabeth realised that Mary would certainly be executed if she were returned to Scotland. If Elizabeth allowed Mary to go free, however, there were three powerful allies to whom Mary could appeal for help – the kings of France and Spain and the Pope. And these Catholic powers might decide to press Mary's claim to the English throne too.

For 18 years, Elizabeth kept Mary in prison in England, unable to convict her and unable to free her. Mary never gave up hope, and repeatedly asked to see Elizabeth, certain that she could convince her of the justice of her case. The two queens never met, however, and Mary turned instead to anyone who promised to help her regain her freedom.

The situation worsened in May 1570 when the Pope excommunicated Elizabeth and issued a papal bull deposing her, whereafter many Roman Catholics in England and abroad regarded Mary as the rightful queen of England. There were several plots to remove Elizabeth and put Mary in her place. As plot after plot was uncovered, the English parliament pressed for Mary's execution, but it was her involvement in the Babington Plot that sealed her fate.

CARLISLE CASTLE
In 1568 Mary was held in Carlisle Castle while Elizabeth tried to decide what to do with her.

TUTBURY CASTLE
Mary was brought to this draughty castle in Staffordshire in February 1569, after the enquiry at York had failed to convict her. During her long imprisonment she was moved from castle to castle, including periods at Chatsworth, Sheffield, Chartley and finally Fotheringhay.

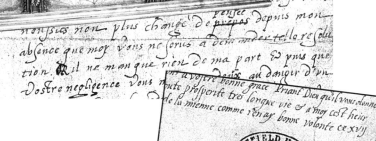

THE BABINGTON PLOT

The Babington Plot was covertly encouraged and organised by Walsingham, Elizabeth's spy master. Antony Babington, a hot-headed young Catholic, was persuaded to head a plot to assassinate Elizabeth and bring in foreign troops to release Mary. All of Mary's letters were intercepted by Walsingham. Now he had the proof he needed! The horsemen, whom Mary thought were coming to rescue her, had been sent to arrest her.

THE CASKET LETTERS

This silver casket, which once belonged to Mary, was produced by Lady Lennox, Darnley's mother, at the enquiry in York into Darnley's death. The letters incriminated Mary but were clearly a forgery.

LETTER TO ELIZABETH

Mary always wrote in French. This letter to Elizabeth was written on 17 April 1583 and pleads for her freedom: 'I do not have any other aspiration than to spend the short time of life which remains to me in greater tranquillity and to use it to your satisfaction and for the common good of this island …' and ended the letter, 'Your very humble and sincerely affectionate good sister and cousin Marie R'.

PASSING THE TIME

Mary never gave up hope of securing her freedom. She spent much of her time in prison writing letters and working embroidery. This piece, called the Bird of America, includes a monogram.

Trial and Execution

WHEN THE Babington Plot was revealed in 1586, Elizabeth could no longer turn a blind eye to her cousin's intrigues. The previous year the English Parliament had passed a law saying that anyone who plotted against the Queen must be tried for treason, so now Elizabeth had to act. The trial took place in October at Fotheringhay

Castle and Mary was found guilty and sentenced to death. Her son James, now 20 years old, did not appeal for clemency. Only Elizabeth could save her.

But Elizabeth was still torn between pressure from her councillors to dispense with Mary once and for all and a reluctance to be responsible for her cousin's death. She did allow a warrant for the execution to be drawn up and even signed it, but afterwards claimed that it was dispatched and acted on without her knowledge and against her will.

Nevertheless the warrant was brought to Fotheringhay and on the evening of 7 February 1587, Mary was told that she would die the following morning. Her response was calm and resigned, 'I thank you for such welcome news. You will do me great good in withdrawing me from this world out of which I am very glad to go.' She divided her money, clothes, jewels and other things among her servants and wrote her final letters.

At 8 o'clock the next morning, Mary was executed at Fotheringhay and buried in Peterborough Cathedral. Although James had not tried to stop his mother's execution, he later achieved what many people from Henry II of France onwards had wanted for Mary: when Elizabeth died in 1603, he became king of both England and Scotland.

TRIAL AT FOTHERINGHAY
During the trial Mary sat alone at one end of the Great Hall at Fotheringhay. The court consisted of earls, barons and knights of the Privy Council. They found Mary guilty of high treason.

MARY'S ROSARY AND PRAYER BOOK
Mary gave this prayer book to Lord Herries, who had sheltered her after the Battle of Langside, but the rosary she carried to her execution. 'I am resolute to die for my religion …', she wrote just before her trial. 'My heart does not fail me …'.